PRICE EXPECTATIONS AND THE BEHAVIOR OF THE PRICE LEVEL

PRICE EXPECTATIONS AND THE BEHAVIOR OF THE PRICE LEVEL

LECTURES GIVEN IN THE
UNIVERSITY OF MANCHESTER

by

R. M. SOLOW

Professor of Economics
Massachusetts Institute of Technology

MANCHESTER UNIVERSITY PRESS

© 1969 Manchester University Press
Published by the University of Manchester at
THE UNIVERSITY PRESS
316–324, Oxford Road, Manchester, M13 9NR

G.B. SBN 7190 0375 X

Printed in Great Britain by Butler & Tanner Ltd, Frome and London

PREFACE

I owe a debt of gratitude to the economists at the University of Manchester for inviting me to give these three Special Lectures in March 1969, for coming to listen to them, and for being so warmly hospitable during my stay there. The lectures are printed substantially as they were delivered. There is a natural tendency to edit, to qualify, to comment on the literature, to add defensive footnotes; but I have resisted it in favor of this less formal, if more vulnerable, tone. I realize that I have not got to the bottom of the expectations hypothesis, or of the other questions about the behavior of the price level discussed in these lectures, but I hope to have contributed to a live discussion that has both theoretical interest and some relevance for economic policy.

I want also to thank Mr. Ira Miller of M.I.T. and Mr. Daniel Luria of the University of Rochester for expert and faithful research assistance, and the National Science Foundation for financial support of the research on which these lectures are based.

ROBERT M. SOLOW

Balliol College, Oxford
April 1969

PRICE EXPECTATIONS AND THE BEHAVIOR OF THE PRICE LEVEL

Robert M. Solow

I

According to the conventional morality, modern capitalist economies want both high output and employment and stable prices. And, according to the conventional wisdom, they can't have both. It is widely accepted that, except for extreme circumstances and with due allowance for lags, a mixed economy can usually squeeze out a little more output if it is prepared to put up with a faster rate of inflation; and it can slow down the going rate of inflation, if it is prepared to sacrifice a certain amount of output and employment. Our jargon is that there is a 'trade-off' between the level of output and the rate of inflation. We mean that there is a curve giving the combinations of level of output and rate of price-change among which the economy can choose by the use of appropriate policy instruments, and that a higher rate of inflation corresponds to a higher level of output. It would be nice to get off the curve in the right direction, to combine higher output with less inflation or even with stable prices. That might perhaps be arranged if wage-making and price-making institutions were changed, or labor mobility increased, or some other fortunate thing were to happen. But in the meanwhile there is that trade-off.

Or is there? The redoubtable Professor Milton Friedman has entered a dissenting view, and he is not alone in holding it. In his Presidential Address to the American Economic Association in December 1967 ('The Role of Monetary Policy', *American Economic Review*, March 1968, page 11) Friedman said: '. . . there is always a temporary trade-off between inflation and unemployment; there is no permanent

1

trade-off. The temporary trade-off comes not from inflation *per se*, but from unanticipated inflation, which generally means from a rising rate of inflation. The widespread belief that there is a permanent trade-off is a sophisticated version of the confusion between "high" and "rising" that we all recognize in simpler forms. A rising rate of inflation may reduce unemployment, a high rate will not.'

My main task in these lectures is to provide a preliminary test of this hypothesis about anticipated inflation, using data for the postwar period in the United States and Great Britain. But before doing that, I must say something about the theoretical background for the hypothesis itself.

It is, in fact, one of those things that it is hard not to believe. Pure theory tells us that any configuration of real quantities in the economy (by 'real quantities', I mean amounts of goods and ratios of prices) is compatible with any rate of inflation of nominal prices. It is only necessary that the inflation be fully anticipated by everyone, so that all the appropriate adjustments have been made in the terms of intertemporal contracts. In particular, if you imagine two isolated island economies tracing out the same real history, but with different steady rates of inflation, then their nominal interest rates must differ by the difference in their rates of inflation so that the real rate of interest is the same in both islands. One would expect the nominal stock of money to be rising at the same rate as the money value of output, and therefore faster in the island with the faster rate of inflation. This points to a minor defect in the story. If there are institutional, legal or technical obstacles to the payment of interest on currency or demand deposits, and if these kinds of money are indispensable for the conduct of business, then inflation has an inescapable real effect. It transfers real income from holders of money to issuers of money, and that may have further real implications; and it may induce people to spend real resources in order to economize on cash balances. But that is hardly a serious hitch; it would be enough if the expectations hypothesis applied to economies that paid interest on demand deposits.

2

If the real situation in the economy is independent of the rate of fully anticipated inflation, then any apparent connection between output and inflation must be the temporary consequence of inaccurate expectations or lags in adjustment. Any constant rate of inflation, high or low, will come to be accurately and confidently expected if it is maintained long enough. When that happens, one must suppose that the economy will revert to the real situation that prevailed before the inflationary episode began. Thus, as Friedman says, steady inflation has no permanent real effects. To have real effects, the rate of inflation must keep increasing, so that expectations can't quite keep up.

To be a bit more precise, let p be the proportional rate of change of the price level, i.e. the rate of inflation. Then the notion that there is a (permanent) trade-off between inflation and real characteristics of the economy boils down to the statement that $p = f(x)$, where x stands for a whole list of the relevant real characteristics like the unemployment rate, the level of output, and any others. The expectations hypothesis says that the correct equation must be

$$p = f(x) + p^*,$$

where p^* is the expected rate of inflation. It must enter with a coefficient of unity because otherwise there would be a relation between p and x even when $p = p^*$, even when the rate of inflation is fully and correctly anticipated; and that is what the expectations hypothesis denies. This way of writing the trade-off equation shows clearly that, under the expectations hypothesis, only $p - p^*$, the unanticipated part of current inflation, has any gearing to the real part of the economy.

The currently expected rate of inflation is not directly observable. It has to be anchored somehow to observable facts, or else the modified trade-off equation tells us very little about any concrete situation. For analytical purposes, it is natural to suppose that the currently expected rate of inflation depends systematically on past observed rates of inflation. Obviously, current expectations depend also on

3

current events, gossip, policy announcements and political prejudices. The only way to handle such factors in theory is to regard them as irregular disturbances to a systematic relation.

The generally favored mechanistic model for the evolution of expectations is what is called the model of 'adaptive expectations'; I have used it in the statistical work to be described later. The model says that $p_{t+1}^* - p_t^* = \theta(p_t - p_t^*)$, with θ a number between zero and one. If the current rate of inflation turns out to be what was expected for this period, then the same rate of inflation will be expected for next period. If the current rate of inflation is greater (or less) than was expected, then the currently expected rate for next period will be revised upward (downward) by a fraction θ of the excess (deficiency). The adaptive expectations model is equivalent to the statement that p_{t+1}^* is a weighted average of p_t, p_{t-1}, p_{t-2}, and so on with weights θ, $\theta(1 - \theta)$, $\theta(1 - \theta)^2$, and so on. The weights attached to past rates of inflation decay geometrically with remoteness in the past; they add up to one. If θ is near zero the weights decay slowly and the system has a long memory. If θ is near one, the weights decay rapidly and the system has a short memory; if $\theta = 1$ only last period's rate of inflation counts. It is clear from this weighted-average property that if the actual rate of inflation becomes and remains constant, the expected rate of inflation will move toward the constant actual rate of inflation and approach it in the limit as time goes on.

I want to combine the expectations-modified trade-off equation with this model of the generation of expectations. But first I generalize the modified trade-off equation to read $p = f(x) + kp^*$, where k is a number between (and including) zero and one. If $k = 0$ we have the original trade-off equation; if $k = 1$ we have the strict expectations hypothesis; if k is in between, we have a situation in which there is partial, but not total, adjustment for anticipated inflation. With adaptive expectations we get

$$p_{t+1}^* = [1 - \theta(1 - k)]p_t^* + \theta f(x_t).$$

This equation shows how the expected rate of inflation (and

4

indirectly the actual rate of inflation) evolves for any time-path of the real variables in the economy. Now suppose that a particular real configuration is reached and maintained for a long time. What happens to the rate of inflation?

First suppose k is less than one, so that there is either no adjustment or partial adjustment, but not complete adjustment, to anticipated inflation. Then $1 - \theta(1 - k)$ is between zero and one; elementary analysis shows that p^* and p, the expected and actual rates of inflation, tend to the same constant, namely $f(x)/(1 - k)$. And this stable permanent rate of inflation is geared to the particular real configuration that is being maintained. There is then a permanent trade-off between the rate of inflation and the components of x.

The strict expectations hypothesis requires that $k = 1$. Then the situation is wholly different. The basic equation becomes $p^*_{t+1} - p^*_t = \theta f(x)$. The actual and expected rates of inflation can be constant if and only if $f(x) = 0$; and in that case the particular rate of inflation that results is not determined by x. Any rate of inflation can be maintained indifferently. This is Professor Friedman's result.

In his simplified presentation, intended only for exposition, x has just one component, the unemployment rate. Then $f(x) = 0$ defines what he calls the 'natural rate of unemployment'. It depends, presumably, on the character of markets, the composition of demand and capacity, the mobility of labor, and other structural characteristics of the economy; and it is the only unemployment rate that is compatible with a constant rate of inflation, indeed with any constant rate of inflation. That is what is meant by saying there is no permanent trade-off between inflation and unemployment. If the government attempts to maintain any other real configuration, a lower unemployment rate, for instance, through fiscal and monetary policy, it can do so only by allowing the rate of inflation to increase perpetually (if $f(x)$ is positive) or by runaway deflation (if $f(x)$ is negative).

I have said that the theoretical foundation of the strict expectations hypothesis is hard not to believe. But in this simple form, at least, the hypothesis has an implication that

5

is not nearly so hard not to believe. Suppose that the 'natural rate of unemployment' is 4%, but the government provides just enough demand in each period to hold the unemployment rate at 3%. Then the theory claims that the rate of inflation (not the price level, but its rate of change) will increase steadily, year after year, without bound.[1] It is perhaps even more startling that, if the unemployment rate is held steadily at 5%, the result must be not only a falling price level, but a price level that falls at an ever-faster rate as time goes on. In the theory, this is necessary to keep the unexpected part of inflation constant, because only that affects the real economy.

No doubt it would be possible to impose 'realistic' qualifications on the theory that would cause it to have rather less drastic implications. Moreover, Professor Friedman believes the process he describes to be a very slow one. Suppose that unemployment is at the 'natural rate' and the price level has been stable for a long time. Now let economic policy generate enough extra demand to drive the price level up at, say, 2% a year and let it do whatever is necessary thereafter to keep the price level rising at that rate. Then Friedman agrees that unemployment will fall initially (and output will rise) and he estimates, informally, that unemployment might continue to fall for two to five years, presumably because of other lags.

At that point the movement begins to be reversed, so presumably unemployment remains below the 'natural rate' for a while longer. Indeed, there seems to be no reason in principle why unemployment should ever rise above the 'natural rate' unless the dynamics of expectations are such as to cause the expected rate of inflation to go higher than 2% a year. If that does not happen, and it will not happen under adaptive expectations, the unemployment rate will simply return to the natural rate when full adjustment to 2% inflation is completed, and Professor Friedman ventures the judgment that full adjustment might take a couple of decades. So slow a process might be difficult to observe in data; and at that pace the adventure might strike you as

[1] This point has been made and emphasized by James Tobin.

worthwhile. It is only fair to point out, however, that at the end of the adjustment process the economy is adapted to a 2% annual rate of inflation. If it ever wants to get back to price stability, it will have to undergo a symmetric process of deflation, with unemployment above the 'natural rate' for the same long period of time.

One way to test the strict expectations hypothesis is to estimate a modified trade-off equation of the form

$$p = f(x) + kp^*,$$

to see if k is in the neighborhood of one; and that is what I have done. That procedure requires an observable proxy for p^* and I have used the adaptive expectations model to provide one. The vehicle of the test is thus an equation to explain the behavior of the price level. I would not defend mine as the last word on the subject, but if it is anywhere in the ball park it will probably serve my main purpose. Perhaps I should say that my initial expectation was that k would turn out to be close to one but that θ would turn out to be very small. That would have left me with a picture much like Professor Friedman's, but with the practical dilemma that I have described: if the temporary trade-off between output and inflation lasts a very long time, it might be irresistible to play on it, and leave the next generation with the problem of getting the rate of inflation back down again, so that it can start over. In fact, I came out with a somewhat different result.

The price index whose rate of change I have tried to explain is that for private domestic nonfarm business product. It seems clear enough that a very inclusive price index is to be preferred, because the expectations hypothesis is fundamentally macroeconomic. There is no reason to believe in the existence of a 'natural level of output' of shoes, or even of manufactures as a whole. On the other hand, it seemed sensible to exclude government product because its recorded price has such a large element of convention, to exclude farm product because agricultural prices have been subject to varying amounts and kinds of support, and to exclude the

7

product of households and nonprofit institutions because it too is not marketed on ordinary business principles. What is left is still pretty broad. It is an index of market prices, not of unit factor costs; I shall comment on this fact later.

Call the level of the index P_t in quarter t. Then my dependent variable is $p_t = (P_t - P_{t-4})/P_{t-4}$. The rate of change in any quarter is the proportional change since the same quarter a year ago; therefore, successive rates of change overlap. This has the unfortunate effect that the 'true' residuals from an explanatory equation will be autocorrelated. On the other hand it has the advantage of eliminating seasonality cheaply, and of reducing the substantial amount of noise in quarter-to-quarter price changes.

I constructed a number of artificial series to do duty as p_t^*, the expected rate of inflation in quarter t. According to the model of adaptive expectations, $p_{t+1}^* = (1 - \theta)p_t^* + \theta p_t$. So p_t^* satisfies a first-order difference equation. For a given choice of θ, a whole time series of p_t^* can be constructed by iteration, starting with a single initial value and using the observed time series of p_t as raw material. I have done this for $\theta = 0 \cdot 1, 0 \cdot 2$, up to $0 \cdot 9$. The extreme case $\theta = 0$ is the case of a constant expected rate of inflation, independent of observed rates; the other extreme, $\theta = 1 \cdot 0$ is the case in which the expected rate of inflation is last quarter's observed rate of inflation. For an initial value to start the process off I chose $p^* = 0$ in 1929. Since I use the resulting series only for post-war years, the choice of an initial value is unimportant; its effect on the calculated p^* series has worn off by then.

(I have mentioned that adaptive expectations is equivalent to the statement that p^* is an infinite weighted average of all past p with geometrically decaying weights. To check the sensitivity of my results to this particular assumption, I experimented with the possibility that p^* is a 20-period or a 10-period weighted average of past p's, with weights falling linearly to zero. The results were statistically a bit less good than with adaptive expectations, but yielded qualitatively similar implications.)

I come now to the 'real' determinants of p, the elements of

8

the vector x in the earlier notation. It would take too long to describe all of the various experiments I tried; but some of the hypotheses eventually excluded are interesting enough to mention in passing. In general, one expects the rate of change of the price level to depend on current and recent changes in unit costs, and on the supply–demand balance in the current period and the recent past. The two cost elements I considered explicitly were unit labor costs and farm prices. Because P is a market price index, I experimented with the introduction of the rate of change of the indirect tax burden (exclusive of property taxes) per unit of real output, but it cut no statistical ice at all.

Unit labor cost (ULC) is the wage bill per unit of real output, and ulc is a series of overlapping four-quarter proportional changes. Lags did not help, so I have used current ulc. Now $ULC = W.R$, where W is a money wage rate and R is labor requirements per unit of output, the reciprocal of output per manhour. Approximately, then, $ulc = w + r$. One can imagine circumstances in which the price response to a change in unit labor cost will differ according as it reflects a change in the money wage or in unit labor requirements. (One can more easily imagine circumstances in which only ulc counts; but it is at least possible that changes in W and R are thought to have different implications about the future.) I have introduced w and r as separate variables; it is always open to the regression to give them the same coefficient. A further case can be made that prices will not reflect transitory changes in productivity to the same extent that they reflect permanent changes in productivity.[1] I was not anxious to work out a measure of permanent productivity change; but I have experimented with $\bar{r}$, the rate of change of a five-quarter moving average of R, centered on the current quarter. (This is merely a smoothing device, to iron out very short-run fluctuations in productivity.)

Agricultural commodities are an input into nonfarm pro-

[1] See O. Eckstein and G. Fromm: 'The Price Equation', *American Economic Review*, December 1968. I had seen an earlier draft of this paper when I was doing my own work, and learned much from it.

duction, so it is natural to include the rate of change of farm prices as a determinant of p from the cost side. No spurious correlation of a total with part of itself is involved in this, because the price index being explained is for nonfarm product. Initially I worked with the four-quarter proportional change of the price index for farm product $(=f)$ as an independent variable. It gave good results, but a modification seemed to work better. The share of farm product in total product decreased irregularly during the postwar period from about 7% to about 4%. It is plausible to assume, therefore, that a given change in f would have a smaller effect on p late in the period than early. I smoothed the share of farm product in total product to fall along a straight line and multiplied each value of f_t by the corresponding smoothed weight. The new series $fs_t = (a - bt)f_t$, where a and b were chosen to make $a - bt$ fall from 7% in 1948 to 4% in 1966.

So far I have mentioned only cost factors. The most suitable measure of demand pressure seemed to be the index of capacity utilization (CU) published by the Wharton School at the University of Pennsylvania. It is available quarterly for the whole postwar period, and its coverage extends beyond manufacturing to include public utilities and service industries. There seemed to be no advantage in using this index with a short lag, but a different sort of modification proved to be worthwhile. One can argue that p may well be insensitive to CU for small variations in capacity utilization around some norm, but not for major variations in either direction. I incorporated this sort of nonlinear effect by the following device. The norm for CU is its average value during the whole sample period, which was 88·5%. Define a nonlinear index of capacity utilization (NCU) by the equation

$$NCU = \frac{(CU - 88\cdot5)^2}{100} \, \text{sgn} \, (CU - 88\cdot5)$$

That is, NCU is $(CU - 88\cdot5)^2/100$ when CU exceeds 88·5, and $-(CU - 88\cdot5)^2$ when CU is less than 88·5. There are many other ways to accomplish the same thing, and in particular the upward and downward effects need not be symmetrical. But this is as far as I have gone; and I have not experimented with lags on NCU.[1] It might be worth doing for its own sake, but it could hardly change the character of my basic results. (The nature of NCU is shown schematically in the diagram.)

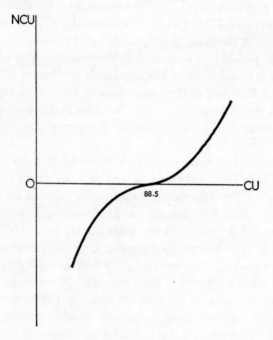

It is perhaps worth mentioning that this way of handling the pressure of demand on capacity does not require any particular presumption about the main determinants of aggregate demand. Whether private spending is moved mainly by changes in income, in money balances, or in assets and incomes generally, any effect on prices must be transmitted through the supply–demand balance and not through the luminiferous ether. I am not neutral on that question, but this method of explaining the behavior of prices is.

The remaining explanatory variables are a pair of

[1] I did experiment with centering NCU around higher and lower values of CU, but 88·5 worked a bit better.

dummies to account for special circumstances. No mechanical model is likely to give a satisfactory explanation of price behavior during the Korean War. Too much depended on expectations left over from the price-control experience of the Second World War, and on the fact that Congress actually passed a price-control act which was not invoked by the President until 1951. I have deliberately avoided doing anything subtle, but have merely introduced a dummy variable called K which is zero except in the four quarters of 1951, when it is equal to one. The regression coefficient of K thus estimates that part of the proportionate increase of the price index in any quarter of 1951 over its value in the same quarter of 1950 that is to be attributed to the special circumstances of the Korean War.

The second dummy variable is likely to be more controversial. It is intended to catch any possible effect on price behavior of the informal incomes policy carried on in the U.S. since 1962. The dummy variable is called G (for Guideposts) and it is zero until the second quarter of 1962, after which it is equal to one. Its regression coefficient estimates the amount by which four-quarter price increases after 1962 fell short of what might have been expected on the basis of the other determinants of the rate of inflation. I imagine that a more subtly tailored dummy variable would perform better and more accurately. But that is a dangerous game to play — a clever man can explain everything with a nice selection of dummy variables — so I have avoided playing it.[1]

My final equation is:

$$p = \text{constant} + a_1 w + a_2 \tilde{r} + a_3 fs + a_4 NCU + a_5 K + a_6 G + a_7 p^*(\theta)$$

where $p^*(\theta)$ is a series for the 'expected rate of inflation' calculated on the hypothesis of adaptive expectations with the parameter value θ. The ordinary least-squares regression estimates and their t-statistics are shown in Table 1 for $\theta = 0{\cdot}0, 0{\cdot}1, 0{\cdot}2, \ldots, 0{\cdot}9, 1{\cdot}0$.

There is quite a lot to be said about these estimates; and

[1] G may well be catching other influences in addition to, or instead of, the Guideposts.

TABLE 1

Regression Coefficients and t-statistics for Alternative Series $p^*(\theta)$

Value of θ	Constant	w	$\bar{r}$	f_S	NCU	K	G	$p^*(\theta)$	Standard error of estimate	R^2
0·0	·0036 (·687)	·5518 (6·225)	·3566 (4·419)	·0942 (·484)	−·0038 (·597)	·0194 (3·601)	−·0045 (1·812)	—	·0078	·8152
0·1	·0017 (·381)	·4094 (5·030)	·4702 (6·442)	·5514 (2·889)	·0019 (·354)	·0157 (3·353)	·0018 (·741)	·3734 (4·925)	·0067	·8659
0·2	·0052 (1·279)	·3309 (4·310)	·3995 (6·323)	·6706 (3·835)	·0072 (1·379)	·0174 (4·141)	−·0001 (·066)	·3743 (6·573)	·0061	·8896
0·3	·0059 (1·539)	·2834 (3·787)	·3142 (5·246)	·7153 (4·304)	·0095 (1·899)	·0166 (4·168)	−·0018 (·949)	·3839 (7·420)	·0058	·9006
0·4	·0061 (1·622)	·2492 (3·342)	·2495 (4·180)	·7262 (4·498)	·0107 (2·183)	·0147 (3·755)	−·0028 (1·588)	·4029 (7·838)	·0056	·9057
0·5	·0061 (1·664)	·2206 (2·948)	·2029 (3·372)	·7264 (4·597)	·0115 (2·367)	·0125 (3·201)	−·0035 (2·007)	·4292 (8·113)	·0055	·9088
0·6	·0062 (1·704)	·1949 (2·597)	·1685 (2·783)	·7233 (4·673)	·0120 (2·502)	·0103 (2·655)	−·0039 (2·285)	·4591 (8·368)	·0054	·9117
0·7	·0062 (1·747)	·1720 (2·294)	·1426 (2·354)	·7167 (4·736)	·0123 (2·599)	·0085 (2·186)	−·0042 (2·471)	·4889 (8·636)	·0054	·9146
0·8	·0063 (1·793)	·1531 (2·052)	·1239 (2·054)	·7044 (4·770)	·0123 (2·655)	·0071 (1·827)	−·0043 (2·593)	·5151 (8·909)	·0053	·9175
0·9	·0063 (1·835)	·1392 (1·882)	·1117 (1·869)	·6844 (4·756)	·0121 (2·663)	·0061 (1·595)	−·0043 (2·661)	·5352 (9·171)	·0052	·9201
1·0	·0063 (1·869)	·1312 (1·793)	·1056 (1·788)	·6558 (4·678)	·0116 (2·616)	·0057 (1·493)	−·0043 (2·681)	·5477 (9·407)	·0051	·9224

I shall come back to them later. For the present, I am interested only in the expectations hypothesis. It is clear that the introduction of $p*$ does help quite a lot, by tightening up the fit and making sense of the farm-price and capacity-utilization variables. So far as the multiple correlation coefficients go, the higher the value of θ the better; $p*(1) = p_{t-1}$ does best of all. That would speak for a very short memory-span; it says that the current expected rate of inflation is the four-quarter increase actually observed last quarter. But there are good reasons for not reading the correlation coefficients uncritically. In the first place, most of the improvement in fit is already in hand by the time $\theta = 0.4$ or 0.5. The reduction in unexplained variance as θ goes from 0.5 to 1.0 is rather small. Secondly, some of that reduction may well be spurious. When $\theta = 1.0$, I am correlating one four-quarter price increase with an overlapping four-quarter change that has three quarters in common with the first. It is no wonder that the fit is pretty good. Finally, the coefficients of w and $\bar{r}$, the rates of change of money wage rates and smoothed unit labor requirements, seem to make more sense for small or intermediate values of θ; 0.4 looks like a good tentative compromise.

Whatever value of θ we choose, however, the coefficient of $p*(\theta)$ is seen to be considerably less than unity. Over the whole range of θ, the coefficient of $p*$ ranges only from 0.37 to 0.55 with a standard error in the neighborhood of 0.06. (The only-to-be-expected serial correlation of the residuals makes the standard errors suspect, but hardly enough to affect that conclusion. For an alternative method of estimation, see Appendix Note 1.

These estimates offer no support whatever to the expectations hypothesis in its strict form. On the contrary, they imply the existence of a permanent trade-off surface whose coefficients can be read from Table 1 by dividing the impact coefficients in each line by the corresponding value of one-minus-the-coefficient-of-$p*$. It follows that the immediate effect of a change in any determinant of p is considerably smaller than its ultimate effect, so the long-run trade-off is

14

less favorable than the short-run. With $\theta = 0.4$, for example, if money wage rates begin to rise 1% a year faster, prices will rise only $\frac{1}{4}$% a year faster at once; but as expectations adjust, the rate of inflation eventuallly rises to become a little more than $\frac{4}{10}$% a year faster than it had been before the acceleration in money wage rates. But the permanent trade-off remains, at least so far as one can tell from the analysis of a 20-year time series. This is perhaps not long enough to do justice to a process as slow as the one Friedman describes; but, as I have remarked, that slow a process makes no dent at all in the practical significance of the trade-off surface for economic policy.

One is driven to ask: How can it be? How can so simple a consequence of economic rationality fail? I don't think it will do just to say that the mechanistic model of adaptive expectations is inadequate to represent what happens in the world. That is no doubt true, but it would account for a poor fit — which we do not have — rather than a clear refutation of the hypothesis — which we do have.

It seems more likely to me that the expectations hypothesis asks more of economic rationality than it can deliver. I can believe that a 10% annual rate of inflation, maintained steadily, will eventually become built into expectations just as the hypothesis describes. But it is not clear that this requires me to believe that a sequence of mostly small, irregularly varying, rates of inflation is fed into the economic system's memory in the same way to produce an expected rate of inflation.

As an alternative, I have made a nonlinear transformation of $p^*(\theta)$ exactly as in the case of capacity utilization. That is to say, I define $np^*(\theta) = (p^*(\theta) - m(\theta))^2 \, \text{sgn} \, (p^*(\theta) - m(\theta))$, where $m(\theta)$ is the mean of $p^*(\theta)$ in the sample period. In words, np^* is the squared deviation of p^* from its average value, with the sign of the deviation attached. The underlying notion is that small deviations of the 'expected rate of inflation' from its average are 'hardly worth adjusting to'; but deviations of a certain size do require and get attention. This is not a fully satisfactory way of allowing a *de*

15

TABLE 2

Regression Coefficients and t-statistics for Alternative Series np^* (θ)

Value of θ	Constant	w	$\bar{r}$	f_s	NCU	K	G	$np^*(\theta)$	Standard error of estimate	R^2
0·1	·0149 (3·550)	·3485 (4·810)	·4823 (7·637)	·6322 (3·848)	·0058 (1·168)	·0202 (4·994)	−·0003 (·180)	13·1713 (7·146)	·0059	·8972
0·2	·0158 (4·044)	·3107 (4·529)	·4433 (7·710)	·5668 (3·840)	·0062 (1·362)	·0233 (6·134)	−·0024 (1·357)	8·5815 (8·272)	·0055	·9106
0·3	·0139 (3·319)	·3332 (4·508)	·4057 (6·601)	·6588 (3·934)	·0071 (1·417)	·0196 (4·827)	−·0033 (1·786)	10·2003 (7·038)	·0059	·8958
0·4	·0150 (3·910)	·2924 (4·242)	·3646 (6·499)	·5318 (3·673)	·0065 (1·432)	·0205 (5·489)	−·0039 (2·290)	8·0631 (8·397)	·0054	·9120
0·5	·0149 (3·817)	·2811 (3·962)	·3304 (5·782)	·5457 (3·684)	·0073 (1·555)	·0173 (4·549)	−·0045 (2·604)	8·6891 (8·130)	·0055	·9090
0·6	·0152 (3·801)	·2652 (3·614)	·3023 (5·178)	·5680 (3·736)	·0082 (1·704)	·0139 (3·551)	−·0051 (2·869)	9·4475 (7·869)	·0056	·9060
0·7	·0156 (3·823)	·2494 (3·296)	·2807 (4·712)	·5851 (3·768)	·0090 (1·829)	·0107 (2·639)	−·0055 (3·069)	10·1910 (7·660)	·0057	·9035
0·8	·0159 (3·834)	·2383 (3·071)	·2667 (4·399)	·5872 (3·728)	·0094 (1·890)	·0082 (1·938)	−·0058 (3·189)	10·7167 (7·477)	·0058	·9013
0·9	·0160 (3·797)	·2353 (2·980)	·2610 (4·245)	·5680 (3·584)	·0094 (1·859)	·0066 (1·512)	−·0059 (3·221)	10·8782 (7·302)	·0058	·8991

minimis principle to operate, not least because the quadratic transform requires that very large deviations call forth over-adjustment. But a more satisfactory procedure would be much more laborious; and this one may tell us something. Table 2 gives regression estimates with np^* replacing p^* as an explanatory variable. The case $np^*(0)$ is the same as the first row of Table 1; the case $np^*(1)$ was omitted by accident.

It is clear from Table 2 that goodness of fit provides only the most tenuous basis for choosing a value of θ. As it happens the correlation is highest for $\theta = 0.4$ and falls off in both directions. But the margin is too small to be taken very seriously. It is quite possible that a less casual approach to the problem of nonlinearity in expectations would give better discrimination among parameter values.

The short-run impact coefficients in Table 2 appear to be reasonable and reasonably well estimated. There is no simple way of passing to long-run coefficients; the point of Table 2 is that the permanent trade-offs for a maintained rate of inflation depend on the particular rate of inflation being maintained. The question one can ask is this: if the trade-off equation is written $p = f(x) + g(p^*)$, at what value of p^* is $g'(p^*) = 1$? That is, at what steady rate of inflation does this trade-off equation behave *locally* as if the strict expectations hypothesis were true? For the case $\theta = 0.4$, the answer is: when the steady rate of inflation is about $8\frac{1}{2}\%$ a year (or when the steady rate of deflation is about 4% a year). This is some distance outside the actual range of experience of the United States. Precisely for that reason, this estimate can hardly be taken literally.

But I think there is a message: whatever may be true of Latin-American-size inflations or even smaller perfectly steady inflations, under the conditions that really matter—irregular price increases with an order of magnitude of a few percent a year—there is a trade-off between the speed of price increase and the real state of the economy. It is less favorable in the long run than it is at first. It may not be 'permanent'; but it lasts long enough for me.

II

The estimated trade-off equations just described have implications that go behond the strict expectations hypothesis.
Before discussing them, however, I want to describe some
similar experiments with British data. I have to admit that I
am less satisfied with the British results than with the American,
for a number of reasons.

In the first place, I did not set out to find the best compact
description of British price-level behavior that I could. I
really wanted something that I could compare with the
American results. So my British equation is simply patterned
on the American equation, with only the smallest modification.

Secondly, I have no general acquaintance with the British
statistics, and therefore no feeling about the appropriateness
of the data I have used for the use to which I have put them.

Thirdly, so far as I could tell, quarterly time series of the
sort I want do not go back much earlier than 1956. I will
therefore describe the results of an investigation of annual
data covering the years 1948–66. I have also done the same
kind of analysis on the quarterly data from 1956 to 1966; and
the quarterly results are in many respects not consistent with
the annual results. This suggests, on the face of it, the possibility that the price level behaved according to different rules
before 1956 and after. But this suggestion is not confirmed by
analysis of the annual data restricted to the years 1956–66. I
am left with the uneasy feeling that there is something
peculiar about the quarterly figures; but at least I can tell
you what I have found.

In the annual exercise, the dependent variable is the year-
to-year proportional change in the price index for final
product. This is a factor-cost index, as I understand it, so I
need not worry about the indirect tax burden as an explanatory variable.[1] Artificial series for $p^*(\theta)$, the 'expected rate of

---

[1] On the assumption, perhaps too pat, that excise taxes are largely
passed forward.

inflation' were produced by iteration from initial conditions, just as before. There is a difference, however. With American data, I was able to start the calculation of p^* so long before the start of the sample period that the choice of an initial 'expected rate of inflation' was utterly washed out of that part of the series actually used in the regressions. In the case of Britain, the price index is not available before 1948, so the iteration must begin with the sample period. The trouble is that other price indexes were moving quite erratically just before 1948, so there was no clear choice for the initial expectation. For each value of θ between 0·1 and 0·9, I calculated three separate series for p^*, one beginning with an expected rate of inflation in 1948 equal to ·02, one beginning with ·04, and one beginning with ·08. Fortunately, the regressions come out much the same, whichever starting value is used, though the series of course differ in the early years.

Unit labor cost is defined as the wage bill divided by real GDP, and ulc is the annual proportional change in ULC. I made an attempt to factor changes in ULC into a change in wage rates and a change in unit labor requirements. But to do so, I had to assume that hours worked per man in the whole economy moved like hours worked per man in manufacturing. In any case, the attempt failed. The regression coefficients were senseless; and I conclude that the data are simply insufficient. Regressions with ulc as a determinant of p made excellent sense.

As a second cost-side determinant I introduced the rate of change of the index of prices of imported raw materials; I shall call the index M and its rate of change m.

From the demand side, I wanted an economy-wide index of capacity utilization. In fact, the only inclusive measure of pressure on capacity that seems to be available for the whole period is Frank Paish's. It is fundamentally a measure of unemployment, i.e. of pressure in the labor market, and that is not what I am after. Still, I have used it, *faute de mieux*. But as it happens, in the annual regressions, CU thus defined appears insignificantly and usually with the wrong sign. So I have dropped it, with little or no loss in goodness of fit. To

19

that extent, my findings confirm the view frequently expressed (by Robert Neild and others) that the British price level is insensitive to demand pressures and primarily cost-determined.

It is not quite so simple as that. When the dependent variable is a series of overlapping four-quarter changes in the price of final product, and the sample period begins in 1956, CU does enter with the right sign, and significantly. The quarterly equations differ in other ways as well; I will come to that soon. In any case, the role of demand pressure remains a bit of a puzzle.

The failure of CU as measured to enter into the annual regressions does not mean that changes in the price level are insensitive to demand pressure, but only that the influence of demand is exercised through changes in ULC. Tight labor markets will presumably drive up money wages and this will be felt in the rate of change of prices in the absence of any compensating increase in productivity. As I have said, Paish's measure of CU is a labor-market measure; and this may explain my failure to detect any independent effect on prices over and above that mediated through ulc. (Since my statistical work was completed, Messrs. Briscoe, O'Brien and Smyth, of Birmingham, have produced some alternative inclusive measures of capacity utilization. But they do not go back before 1954 either. Perhaps if their series were extended back to 1948 they could be used as explanatory variables with different results. For their use in quarterly regressions, see Appendix Note 2.)

The only remaining explanatory variables are two dummies. One is called CD (for Cripps Dummy) and is zero except in 1948 and 1949, when it is unity. The other is called LD (for Lloyd Dummy); it is unity in 1961 and zero the rest of the time. They are intended, of course, to catch the effects, if any, of two attempts to talk down the rate of change of prices. Perhaps surprisingly, they both seem to have worked.

The final equation is:

$$p = a_0 + a_1 ulc + a_2 m + a_3 CD + a_4 LD + a_5 p^*(\theta)$$

and the results are given in Table 3. (Once more, the cases $\theta = 0.0$ and 1.0 were omitted inadvertently. Since $p^*(0.1)$ has a coefficient effectively equal to zero, $\theta = 0.0$ would be very like $\theta = 0.1$.)

To the extent that these regressions cast any light on the expectations hypothesis, they cast it in the form of doubt. For low values of θ (the expected rate of inflation generated with a long memory), $p^*(\theta)$ is without statistical significance. It is significant and useful as soon as θ exceeds 0.4. The missing equation with $\theta = 1.0$ ($p_t^* = p_{t-1}$) would presumably give the best fit by a small margin. But in any case, the coefficient of p^* is always close to 0.2. Taken literally, that means that there is a permanent trade-off and its slope is only 25% greater than the short-run instantaneous trade-off (because $1/(1 - 0.2) = 1.25$). In the U.S. regressions, the coefficient of p^* was about 0.4–0.5, so the slopes of the permanent trade-off were nearly twice the slopes of the instantaneous trade-off. But the strict expectations hypothesis requires that the permanent trade-off have infinite slope, and the data do not seem to bear that interpretation at all.

In other respects, the equations of Table 3 seem satisfactory. The fit is good, the coefficients have the right sign and order of magnitude, and appear to be stable. It is interesting that both the Cripps and Lloyd Dummies are significantly negative, with the Cripps effects between three and four times the Lloyd effects in size. I was unable to make a Wilson Dummy work. Perhaps it would do so if the sample period were extended to 1968. Here too it should be remembered that the full effects of any incomes policy on prices include an effect through wage changes and the coefficients of *ulc*. But in any case, this sort of fishing expedition is only the beginning of any attempt to estimate the effectiveness of incomes policies.

I will not give a complete catalogue of my trials with quarterly data for the U.K., but in all honesty I must give some picture of the results. Those variables in the rate-of-change form are four-quarter overlapping proportional changes; the sample period extends from the third quarter of 1957 to the fourth quarter of 1966.

21

TABLE 3

Regression Coefficients and t-statistics for Alternative Series p^* (θ) : Great Britain, annual data

Value of θ	Constant	ulc	m	CD	LD	$p^*(\theta)$	Standard error at estimate	R^2
0·1	·0069 (·594)	·6358 (10·405)	·0839 (8·853)	−·0399 (5·246)	−·0216 (3·182)	·0034 (·011)	·0061	·9610
0·2	·0039 (·579)	·6294 (10·333)	·0850 (8·991)	−·0408 (5·379)	−·0205 (2·997)	·0901 (·495)	·0060	·9618
0·3	·0024 (·461)	·6209 (10·475)	·0866 (9·371)	−·0418 (5·675)	−·0191 (2·847)	·1435 (1·044)	·0058	·9642
0·4	·0015 (·358)	·6112 (10·841)	·0884 (10·024)	−·0429 (6·140)	−·0177 (2·768)	·1795 (1·635)	·0055	·9681
0·5	·0012 (·339)	·6005 (11·391)	·0902 (10·942)	−·0438 (6·761)	−·0164 (2·259)	·2005 (2·259)	·0051	·9726
0·6	·0013 (·453)	·5886 (12·022)	·0917 (12·055)	−·0446 (7·495)	−·0155 (2·843)	·2092 (2·889)	·0047	·9770
0·7	·0018 (·720)	·5750 (12·623)	·0930 (13·307)	−·0453 (8·314)	−·0147 (2·962)	·2109 (3·521)	·0043	·9808
0·8	·0024 (1·141)	·5599 (13·113)	·0940 (14·633)	−·0459 (9·179)	−·0142 (3·114)	·2091 (4·140)	·0039	·9839
0·9	·0031 (1·700)	·5438 (13·453)	·0949 (15·988)	−·0464 (10·066)	−·0137 (3·272)	·2063 (4·739)	·0036	·0984

In these regressions, the change in prices of imported raw materials was statistically insignificant. This is perhaps not surprising, since the quarterly sample excludes the Korean War, when most of the action from that source took place. The Lloyd Dummy was also insignificant (and of course the Cripps Dummy can play no part). On the other hand, the Paish index of capacity utilization did enter consistently and significantly, with the right sign. A fair example of the results is the equation for $\theta = 0 \cdot 7$, which happens to give the best fit. It is:

$$p = \begin{array}{cccc} -0 \cdot 2325 & + 0 \cdot 0812 ulc & + 0 \cdot 00243 CU & + 0 \cdot 8085 p^*; \\ (4 \cdot 770) & (1 \cdot 630) & (4 \cdot 844) & (8 \cdot 113) \end{array}$$

the standard error of estimate was $0 \cdot 0051$ and $R^2 = 0 \cdot 8436$.

The impact coefficient of ulc is much smaller in this equation than in the corresponding annual equation: $0 \cdot 0812$ against $0 \cdot 5750$. This is partially explained by the fact that the implied long-run coefficients are much closer together— roughly $0 \cdot 42$ against $0 \cdot 73$—and partially by the fact that CU, reflecting labor-market conditions as it does, undoubtedly picks up some of the effect that would be attributed in its absence to ulc. (I should add that provision for some lags in ulc changed the picture in detail, but not in any important way.)

The other important observation is that the coefficient of p^* is much larger in the quarterly regressions—$0 \cdot 8$ against $0 \cdot 2$—and in fact not very far from one. These equations are thus much more favorable to the strict expectations hypothesis.

This led me to re-run the annual regressions for the period 1956–1966 only. The result for $\theta = 0 \cdot 7$ was:

$$p = \begin{array}{ccccc} 0 \cdot 0038 & +0 \cdot 5816 ulc & +0 \cdot 0984 m & -0 \cdot 0169 LD & +0 \cdot 1803 p^* \\ (0 \cdot 978) & (10 \cdot 207) & (2 \cdot 739) & (3 \cdot 357) & (1 \cdot 395) \end{array}$$

with a standard error of estimate of $0 \cdot 0037$ and $R^2 = 0 \cdot 9568$. These coefficients differ hardly at all from those in the corresponding row of Table 3, so there is no case for a change in price-formation behavior after 1956.

23

I have no ready explanation for the inconsistency of quarterly and annual regression coefficients. My inclination is to wonder if the quarterly figures are very good. This inclination is reinforced by one by-product of the quarterly regressions. I have mentioned that one would expect the residuals from regressions involving four-quarter overlapping changes to be serially correlated, precisely because successive four-quarter changes have three quarters of history in common. This happens in the American data. But the residuals from the quarterly regression just quoted have a Durbin–Watson statistic of 2·37, which suggests slight negative serial correlation if anything. This may just reflect a badly specified equation; but it may also correspond to something peculiar in the underlying data.

This difficulty with the British equation, whatever its source, takes some of the bloom off my desire to make comparisons between the rules of price-level formation in the United States and Great Britain. Nevertheless, I am prepared to go some way down that path.

The first question is the extent to which the price level is sensitive to the pressure of demand on capacity, over and above any effect from the cost-side, especially the wage side. The conventional view is that the price-level is almost completely cost-determined in Great Britain, and is certainly less sensitive to direct demand conditions than in the United States. My results generally confirm this view. You have already seen that the Paish index of economy-wide capacity utilization doesn't work at all in annual regressions for the whole of the postwar period or for the sub-period since 1956. The index itself is probably deficient for my purpose; but that only makes this a tentative, rather than firm, conclusion.

In the quarterly regressions, where CU does play a significant role, another interesting fact emerges. In a trade-off equation of the form $p = f(x) + kp^*$, the root of $f(x) = 0$ does not have the overwhelming importance it does in Friedman's theory $(k = 1)$; but even when k is less than one, $f(x) = 0$ does describe the real situations compatible with a stable price level when expectations have fully adjusted to price level stability. The quarterly equation I have quoted, with $\theta = 0.7$, leads to

$$0.0812ulc + 0.00243CU = 0.2325$$

for $p = p^* = 0$. Suppose unit labor costs were constant ($ulc = 0$): what level of the Paish index would be compatible with stable prices? The answer is: about 95·7%. This is to be compared with the average level of the Paish index from 1957 to 1966, which was 96·3%. So if unit labor costs had been constant (a big if) price stability could have been achieved with a reduction in the Paish index of less than one percentage point. According to the implied permanent trade-off equation, with expectations fully adjusted, an extra 0·6% on the Paish index adds about $\frac{3}{4}$% a year to the rate of inflation. In fact, during the decade beginning in 1957, the price index for final product rose at an average rate of 2·55% a year. The permanent trade-off equation attributes 0·75% a year to the fact that the Paish index averaged 96·3% instead of 95·7%. ULC actually rose at an average annual rate of 3·52% during the period; that was responsible for about 1·49% of the annual increase in prices, twice the amount imputed to CU. (The remaining 0·3% a year presumably comes from the fact that expectations were not fully adjusted; and the period began with expectations of rising prices.)

I would not want these calculations taken too seriously. I have doubts about the equation, and about the fitness of the Paish index as a measure of demand pressure in the goods market. (In particular it probably attributes some labor-market effects to the goods market.) Moreover, these derived calculations depend much too much on the last decimal point in each regression coefficient.

I would not want these calculations misunderstood either. To say that the rise in ULC was responsible for twice as much of the post-1957 inflation as the excess of CU over 95·7% is not to apportion blame. It is open to anyone to argue that it would have been 'right' for unit labor costs to rise as fast as they did or faster, and for business to have absorbed the cost increase at the expense of profits. Furthermore, it would be a valid observation that $\frac{1}{2}\%$ of GDP is not to be sneezed at. Even if the quarterly equation were accurate, which I have doubted, it could not hope to tell anyone what should have happened; the most it can do is say what would have happened if circumstances had been different but behavior parameters the same.

In the U.S. the independent role of demand pressure is more securely estimated, I think. The equation with $\theta = 0.4$ from Table 1 reads:

$$p = \begin{array}{l} 0.0061 + 0.2492w + 0.2495\bar{r} + 0.7262fs \\ + 0.0107NCU + 0.0147K - 0.0028G + 0.4029p* \end{array}$$

where $NCU = (CU - 88.5)^2 \mathrm{sgn}(CU - 88.5)/100$. The natural question to ask here is: suppose unit labor cost is constant (i.e. $w + \bar{r} = 0$), farm prices are constant, it is not 1951, and expectations are completely adapted to stable prices: what level of capacity utilization is consistent with price stability? According to the equation, the answer depends on whether it is before or after the first quarter of 1962. If before, we have to solve

$$0.0061 + 0.0107NCU = 0;$$

if after, we have to solve

$$0.0033 + 0.0107NCU = 0.$$

The answers come out: before 1962, the price level would stabilize with $CU = 81\%$; after 1962 with $CU = 83\%$. The average of CU in 1947–66 was 88.5%.

Now suppose that all the other stipulations (about constant unit labor costs and farm prices) were to hold, but capacity utilization stayed at its postwar average. What rate of inflation would then be consistent with fully adapted expectations? That is, what p is implied by $NCU = 0$ and $p = p*$. The answer is given by $p = 0.0061/(1 - 0.4029)$ or about 1% a year before 1962 and $p = 0.0033/(1 - 0.4029)$ or a bit over $\frac{1}{2}\%$ a year after 1962. Because the particular nonlinear transform of CU is symmetrical around 88.5%, one can say that under pre-1962 conditions steady capacity utilization of 96% would have added 1% a year to the rate of inflation, provided unit labor costs and farm prices could have been held constant. The analogous statement for post-1962 conditions is that the rate of inflation would have been $\frac{1}{2}\%$ higher with the Wharton School capacity utilization index at 94%, than with the index at 88·5%.

The price index for private nonfarm business GNP actually rose at an average annual rate of 2·04% in the sample period. The 'permanent trade-off' between inflation and demand pressure (in product markets) in the United States is thus peculiar. The 'break-even point' is undesirably low. No one would actually enjoy keeping capacity utilization down to 81–83%, but that is what would be required to stabilize prices if unit labor costs and farm prices were constant. On the other hand, even the 'permanent' trade-off appears to be rather flat. A perpetual 1% a year rise in the price level seems like a bargain if it could actually buy a permanent (or even a decade's) increase of something over 5% in the yearly level of output.

But of course this is a pipedream. Capacity utilization of 95% on the Wharton School index corresponds to an unemployment rate in the neighborhood of $3\frac{1}{2}$–$3\frac{3}{4}\%$. In those circumstances, money wage rates will be rising faster than productivity, unit labor costs will be rising, and the rate of inflation will be higher than what is calculated from goods-market considerations alone. Secondly, while I am interested by the fact that my equations seem to pick up visible commodity-market effects from incomes policies, I think it has to be agreed that there is as yet no evidence that these effects can be sustained for a very long period of time under conditions of prolonged demand pressure. So it is perhaps the 'pre-1962' rather than the 'post-1962' trade-off that has to be taken into account.

Nevertheless, if I am to believe my own results—and if I do not, who will?—I have to conclude that even in the United States, changes in the rate of inflation are not violently sensitive to changes in demand pressure, at least not for variations of a few percentage points on either side of the postwar average of the Wharton School index of capacity utilization. This is not utterly inconsistent with the vaguer indications that the British price level is moved mainly from the cost side. (In this connection, I should add that the annual Paish index ranges only from 93·5 to 99·7 during the sample period; the quarterly Wharton School index ranges from 79·6 to 98·6. The greater variability in the American data is no source of satisfaction with economic policy, but it no doubt accounts for the more reliable estimate of demand effects.)

The second comparison one would like to make has to do with the response of price changes to wage changes.

The annual regressions for Britain say that a one-per-centage-point increase in the rate of increase of unit labor costs generates in the same year an increase in the rate of price inflation of about 0·5–0·6 percentage points. The operation of adaptive expectations builds the long-run effect up to about 0·73 percentage points.

For the U.S., I shall take the row of Table 1 with $\theta = 0.4$. This choice is about as good as any. It is the value of θ with the best fit in Table 2; and it has the advantage that the coefficients of w and $\bar{r}$ are identical, so that only the rate of change of unit labor costs $(ulc = w + \bar{r})$ enters into the equation. That equation says that a one-point increase in the rate of change of unit labor costs has the impact effects of raising the rate of price inflation by a quarter of a point. The operation of adaptive expectations eventually builds the effect up to some 0·42 percentage points. This is a consider-ably smaller effect than the British equations detect, both in the short run and the long run. (The quarterly British regressions give results much closer to the American ones, which are also quarterly. I suspect this is more coincidence than anything else; and I have mentioned that I am suspicious of the quarterly data for Britain.)

What should one expect to find here? That depends on the sort of pricing model one believes. Simple competitive pricing gives a well-known result. If output is produced under con-stant returns to scale, then product price must be a function of all the input prices, homogeneous of first degree (because doubling or halving all input prices will leave the least-cost combination of inputs unchanged, and therefore double or halve average and marginal cost). In fact the elasticity of product price with respect to the money wage will be the same as the elasticity of output with respect to labor input. Indeed, if the production function were Cobb-Douglas, then product price would be a Cobb-Douglas function of input prices, with the same constant elasticities as in the production function. The same thing will be true locally even if the production function is not Cobb–Douglas; the elasticities in question will simply not be constants.

A constant-elasticity relation between P and ULC leads to a linear relation between p and ulc, since $Y = cX^a$ implies $y = ax$. The analogy of competitive pricing would lead one to expect the coefficient of ulc or w to be near the observed share of wage income in total business product.

Something similar happens even if output and inputs are not sold in competitive markets. The various degrees of monopoly and monopsony enter as multiplicative constants, as mark-ups; it remains true that the elasticity of product price with respect to the money wage is the same as the elasticity of output with respect to labor input. The big difference is that the share of wages in total output is an indicator of the corresponding elasticity only in the competitive case; otherwise the observed wage share will differ from the technological elasticity in ways that depend on the various degrees of monopoly and monopsony.

In the U.S. case, the long-run coefficient of ulc in the equation for p is 0·42. The share of wages in the appropriate output total is about 58%; there is a considerable but hardly staggering gap between those numbers. In Britain, the long-run coefficient is 0·73, and the wage bill is about 55% of final output less indirect taxes; the discrepancy is about as big as in the U.S. figures, but in the opposite direction. These estimates seem more or less reasonable to me. I would not expect broad price indexes to behave exactly as if they were set by competitive pricing, or even by constant-degree-of-monopoly pricing. It is encouraging if the orders of magnitude are even approximately right.

29

This is perhaps the place to say a word about a purely statistical matter. The estimates I have exhibited were done by single-equation least squares. They are therefore vulnerable to a simultaneous-equations bias. Fortunately there are some qualitative statements about the probable bias that seem plausible.

Most of the independent variables in these regressions are about as exogenous as one ever has any right to expect. The main exception is the rate of change of money wages in the American regression; the change in unit labor cost is an offender in the British regression, for the same reason. If one were writing out a complete system of equations, there would be another in which w was the independent variable, and p or perhaps lagged p would figure among the independent variables, with a positive coefficient less than unity. The usual sorts of considerations suggest that the estimated coefficient of w in the equation for p will have an upward bias. This may explain why the British coefficient comes out so high. Of course, the estimate of the same coefficient from American data seems, if anything, too low. My guess is that the presence of a capacity-utilization variable in the American regression gets rid of some of the bias, perhaps all. (Remember that with quarterly British data CU also figures significantly and the estimated long-run coefficient of ulc drops to $0·42$.)

Actually there is some room for hope that the bias may be very small in the first place. It is arguable that only unit labor costs should appear in the equation: changes in cost are changes in cost, regardless of how they are composed of wage changes and productivity changes. In that case, w and $\bar{r}$ should have approximately equal coefficients. But $\bar{r}$ is certainly exogenous in this model; so if w is much affected by simultaneous-equation bias, this might show itself as a difference in the coefficients of w and $\bar{r}$, with that of w being larger. In the actual regressions, the two coefficients are usually very close, and more often than not the coefficient of w is the smaller.

For rather similar reasons one might expect the coefficient of p^* to be biased upward in these regressions. But that, of

30

course, merely strengthens the important conclusion that the true coefficient is less than one.

The element of raw-materials costs is carried in the American regressions by the rate of change of farm prices, and in the British regressions by the rate of change of a price index of imported raw materials. Both of these can fairly be taken as more or less exogenous, and indeed their estimated coefficients fall in the right range. The rate of change of farm prices in the U.S. regressions is already adjusted for the weight of farm product in total output, so its coefficient ought to be about unity. In fact, the impact coefficients is about 0·72, and the long-run coefficient about 1·2. In the annual regressions for the U.K., the estimated coefficient of import prices is a bit over 0·09 in the short run, rising to about 0·12 in the long run. That is within striking distance of the weight of imported materials in the value of final output.

I can summarize these rather scattered observations briefly. My results seem to confirm the common belief that the British price level is moved mainly by labor costs and the prices of imported raw materials. That doesn't mean that it is insensitive to the pressure of demand, but rather that demand pressure operates primarily through the labor market. In the United States, the independent operation of demand pressure in commodity markets is much more clearly visible. But even there, the slope of the direct trade-off is rather flat although the 'break-even point' is undesirably low. As in Britain, a large part of the inflationary potential of high demand operates through its effect on money wages, transmitted in the normal way into the prices of final output. In both countries there is a definite process of adjustment of expectations to the recent history of the price level. This process is enough to make the long-run trade-off between the rate of inflation and its determinants—including the direct and indirect effects of demand pressure—steeper than the immediate trade-off. But in neither country is the strict expectations hypothesis valid for the sort of time-span considered. The long-run trade-off appears to be real.

I have not commented much on the fact that the data for

both countries show an effect that might reasonably be attributed to informal incomes policies. This effect, such as it is, works over and above any additional influence through wage restraint. I am reluctant to place a lot of weight on this indication of the effectiveness of incomes policies, though I think it is promising enough to justify further work. My own intention has been not so much to arrive at the best possible explanation of changes in the general level of prices as to find an explanation adequate for a test of the expectations hypothesis.

III

The notion that there exist trade-off relations, connecting the rates of change of prices and money wages with real characteristics of the economy, has certain paradoxical implications that have sometimes been noticed. One of them—the apparent failure of the expectations hypothesis over usefully long periods of time—has already been discussed. Another apparent paradox depends on some of the characteristics of empirically fitted trade-off surfaces.

It is well-known that statistical Phillips surfaces—which are trade-off equations with the rate of change of the money wage as the dependent variable—usually or always show a strong back-effect from price changes, perhaps with a short lag. Thus an equation to explain w will have p as an explanatory variable, just as my equations for p have w or ulc on the right-hand side. Typically—maybe even universally— the coefficient of p is less than 1, usually around $\frac{1}{2}$ or even less. This is by itself paradoxical, because it smacks of severe money illusion. It implies that the process of wage determination does not compensate the worker fully for price inflation (and would over-compensate him for price deflation). If the rate of price inflation were to rise by one percentage point and stay there, all other things equal, money wage rates would inflate by only half a point a year faster than they had been doing. Therefore, real wages would rise half a point slower than they had been rising before. If there were no change in the rate at which output per worker were rising, the share of wages in total output would fall steadily. If this story were really so, we would certainly have noticed it.

On the other hand, the price trade-off equations I have been describing all have the rate of change of the money wage as an explanatory variable (or the rate of change of unit labor cost, which comes to the same thing with a given rate of productivity increase.) In all of them, w appears with a coefficient less than one, even in the permanent trade-off

33

equation with fully adapted expectations. The coefficient may be in the neighborhood of the share of wages in output, but that is not very important in the present context.

This seems to lead to the opposite paradox. Imagine an initial situation with unit labor cost constant (i.e. $ulc = 0$) and prices constant. Now let the wage begin to rise at 1% a year, everything else unchanged. The price level will begin to rise, and rise faster as expectations adapt; but eventually, according to the equations, p will stabilize at a value equal to the coefficient of w or ulc in the permanent trade-off equation, therefore less than 1% a year. It appears, therefore, that the real wage will continue to rise. With an unchanged rate of productivity gain, the share of wages will rise steadily.

From the point of view of the wage trade-off, it appears that faster inflation cheats the wage-earner; from the point of view of the price trade-off, it appears that faster inflation cheats the recipient of nonwage income. Yet I imagine most of us suspect that, except in the short run, faster inflation cheats neither group systematically (except the recipients of fixed monetary incomes, who can be neglected for this purpose). What can be happening?

One possible escape from this paradox presents itself immediately: take account of both the wage equation and the price equation. This has to be part of the answer, because it is obviously right to take account of both equations if they both in fact hold. But it is not the whole answer, as one can easily see.

Suppose we think of an economy with stationary productivity, so $w = ulc$; it is easy to make the appropriate modification when output per man is actually rising. Take the simplest sort of permanent trade-off equations:

$$p = a + bw$$
$$w = A + Bp,$$

where a and A are not necessarily constants, but depend on the real configuration of the economy in ways we need not specify now. According to the empirical generalization I mentioned earlier, both b and B are between zero and one.

Now for given values of a and A, these are two linear equations in the two unknowns w and p. They can always be solved for w and p because their determinant is $1 - bB$, which is positive. The unique solution is:

$$p = \frac{a + bA}{1 - bB}$$

$$w = \frac{A + Ba}{1 - Bb},$$

which are both positive if a and A are positive; all combinations of signs are possible. This is the only possible state of steady wage and price inflation corresponding to any particular real configuration of the economy.

Remember that I have assumed productivity to be stationary. In conditions of steady inflation, one would expect the price level and the money wage to be rising at the same rate. Then the real wage and distributive shares would be constant or else would be changing slowly in a direction and at a pace governed by real factors, not by the mere fact of regular inflation.

But the little model tells us that w will be bigger or smaller than p according as $A + Ba$ is greater or smaller than $a + bA$. Indeed, if V is the real wage and v its rate of change,

$$v = w - p = \frac{A(1 - b) - a(1 - B)}{1 - bB},$$

and the real wage rises or falls according as the numerator of that fraction is positive or negative. The behavior of the real wage in regular inflation appears to depend on the parameters of both trade-off equations, and on the particular real configuration in which the model economy is established. For v to be zero, we must have $A(1 - b) = a(1 - B)$ and that would be a coincidence.

So taking account of both trade-off equations gets us somewhere; the rates of wage and price inflation corresponding to any real state of the economy are determined.

The significance of having b and B both less than one is that then the 'equilibrium' rates of inflation are stable. If the product bB were bigger than one, a chance increase of w would induce a rise in p, and that in turn would induce a further rise in w bigger than the initial impulse. The result must be hyperinflation or hyperdeflation, depending on the direction of the original impulse. When bB is less than one, there is leakage, as in a multiplier system with a marginal propensity to spend less than one. An initial impulse sets off a sequence of echoes, but they diminish in size fast enough so that they cumulate only to determinate finite rates of price and wage inflation.

The 'incidence' of inflation depends, as I have said, on all the parameters of both trade-offs, and on the real situation as well. Notice, for instance, that if $b < 1$ and $B = 1$ the stability condition is satisfied, but the steady-state w is necessarily greater than the steady-state p (provided that A is positive, i.e. that the labor market is tight enough to cause the money wage to rise even if the price level were constant.) Thus the real wage is always rising in regular inflation if there is 'money illusion' in the price equation but not in the wage equation. And, of course, if $b = 1$ and $B < 1$, so all the money illusion is in the wage equation, then regular inflation cheats the wage earner and the real wage falls. In the case that seems to correspond to most regression results, we are left with no presumption at all, but only the unsatisfactory implication that regular inflation will cheat one side or the other permanently, except in the improbable case that all the parameters fall out just right. I call this implication unsatisfactory because it does not correspond to common observation. We expect inflation to generate distributional shifts in the short run, but hardly continuing shifts if the inflation becomes regular.

(This line of argument sounds like the strict expectations hypothesis again. Quite so; the analogy is pretty close. The argument that 'rationality requires $b = B = 1$, and therefore in fact it must be true that $b = B = 1$' operates just like the strict expectations hypothesis. Inserted into the trade-off equations, it requires that $p = a + w = w - A$, and therefore that $a + A = 0$. Since a and A depend on real factors, we are back to the Friedman notion of a 'natural rate of un-employment' by a slightly different route.)

So far I have discussed the real wage as if it were nothing more than the casual outcome of a tug-of-war between the money wage and the price level. It is that too, no doubt, and the whole discussion of trade-off equations is intended to elucidate that side of the matter. But presumably the real wage figures also as a non-trivial part of the functioning of the real economy. And since real factors appear in the trade-off equations, the analysis so far has been incomplete. In terms of the simplified model I have been using, it is not enough to say that a and A depend on real factors and, together with the trade-off parameters, determine w, p, and therefore $v = w - p$. It is not enough because the real factors, on which a and A depend, may have to change precisely because the real wage is changing. A complete theory must take that dependence into account.

A complete theory would be a self-contained macroeconomics; I am in no position to offer that. For the particular point at issue, I hope I can get away with a considerably simplified version of a model analyzed in the *Quarterly Journal of Economics* (November 1968) by Joseph Stiglitz and myself.

To begin with, suppose we agree to represent the 'real factors' in both trade-off equations simply by the current level of real output, Y. Obviously, I don't believe that will really do, nor do I expect anyone else to believe it; it is merely an expository simplification. Holding to linear relations, I can write the slightly extended trade-off equation as:

$$p = a + bw + cY$$
$$w = A + Bp + CY.$$

Here c and C are positive coefficients; $-a/c$ and $-A/C$ are, respectively, the level of real output that would stabilize the price level if the money wage were constant, and the money wage if the price level were constant. (I am still imagining productivity to be constant; otherwise replace w by $w + r$, where r is the rate of change of labor requirements per unit of real output.)

As before, these two equations can be solved for p and w because $bB < 1$. One gets

$$p = \frac{a + bA}{1 - bB} + \frac{c + bC}{1 - bB} Y$$

$$w = \frac{A + Ba}{1 - bB} + \frac{C + Bc}{1 - bB} Y$$

and, therefore,

$$v = w - p = (1 - bB)^{-1} \times$$
$$\{[A(1 - b) - a(1 - B)] + [C(1 - b) - c(1 - B)]Y\}$$

This is no more than we had before, except that the dependence on Y is made explicit. Evidently there is one value of Y, which I shall call Y^*, that makes $v = 0$, i.e. one level of real output that causes the money wage and the price level to rise at the same rate, so that the real wage is constant.

It is important to know whether v is an increasing or decreasing function of Y; that is, whether a still higher level of output than Y^*, a tighter economy, would make the real wage rise or fall. A higher level of output makes the money wage rise faster; it also makes the price level rise faster. The real wage will rise if wage inflation accelerates more than price inflation; in the opposite case, a higher level of output will cause the real wage to decline or to rise more slowly, even though money wages and prices both rise more rapidly.

From the equation, v is an increasing function of Y if $C(1 - b)$ exceeds $c(1 - B)$, a decreasing function of Y if the inequality is reversed. I think it is a fair reading of most statistical work in this field that b is probably slightly bigger than B but that C tends to be bigger than c. That judgment translates into the statement that the back-effect of wages on prices is perhaps slightly larger than the reverse effect of prices on wages; and that the pressure of demand drives the rate of inflation more strongly through the labor market than through the market for goods and services. If this is a correct description of the state of affairs, it is hard to extract a clear presumption about the relation of v to Y.

Guesses have been made, of course. Professor Kaldor, for example, holds that wages are more sticky than prices. That

38

is to say, when Y exceeds Y^* margins increase and the real wage falls; when Y is less than Y^*, wage rates tend to be better maintained while margins weaken, so the real wage rises. In this view, v is a decreasing function of Y. (Professor

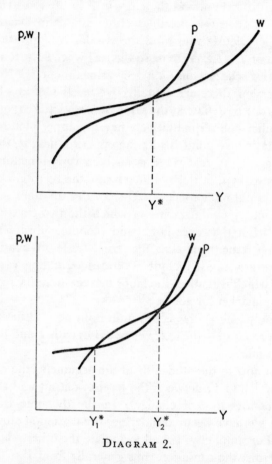

DIAGRAM 2.

Kaldor identifies Y^* with 'full employment', but that definition, if that is what it is, appears to have no particular merit.)

One difficulty with my brief summary of empirical findings is that it refers to a pair of linear trade-off equations, whereas much empirical work, though not all, suggests that both equations may be nonlinear. Many statistical Phillips-curves either assume or conclude that the relation between w and

39

the unemployment rate is hyperbolic; that would be roughly equivalent to making w an increasing, convex function of Y. On the other hand, my own tentative version of the price trade-off equation makes p a nonlinear function of the rate of capacity utilization, and therefore of Y in the short run.

I have drawn two possible configurations in Diagram 2. The upper picture illustrates the Kaldor configuration. To the right of Y^*, p exceeds w, so the real wage falls; to the left of Y^*, w exceeds p. Thus v is a decreasing function of Y. In the lower version, there are actually two levels of Y at which w and p inflate or deflate at the same rate, so that V is constant. The smaller one is qualitatively like the upper picture. The larger stationary point is just the opposite; near it, the rate of change of the real wage is an increasing function of Y. Obviously, then, in this nonlinear case the relation between v and Y is not monotone, but U-shaped. Still other patterns are possible, including some in which the two curves never intersect; but that does not sound economically interesting when one remembers that the 'true' trade-off relations, if there are any, must include several determining variables, some of which will affect the labor market more strongly and some the market for goods.

The only safe course is to retain both possibilities and to consider separately the case where v rises with Y and the case where it falls.

I turn now to the other side of the argument, the relation between Y and V, between the level of output and the real wage (not its rate of change). In the dynamic trade-off relation we have been considering, the causation runs from Y to v. For simplicity, I shall formulate the other relation in static terms; the causation runs generally from V to Y. The real wage is regarded as a determinant of the level of output.

The real wage rate functions macroeconomically in two ways: as a source of income and as an item of cost. Correspondingly, the size of the real wage operates on the level of aggregate output both from the demand side and from the supply side. So the character of its influence may depend on whether demand factors or supply factors predominate.

40

The normal presumption is that aggregate demand in real terms is an increasing function of the real wage rate. For a given amount of output and employment, a higher real wage necessarily redistributes income from other forms toward wages. On the presumption that the marginal propensity to consume wage income is very high, the result will be an increase in real consumption demand. One ought to offset against this upward shift in the consumption function the possibility that the higher real wage reduces the prospective profitability of investment. If it does, the investment schedule may fall at each level of output. The net effect on the combined aggregate demand schedule is moot in principle, but one supposes that the consumption effect will usually outweigh the investment effect. In that case, aggregate demand is an increasing function of the real wage. In circumstances where actual current real output is determined on the demand side, current output and employment will be higher the higher the real wage.

I would not expect this relation to be very strong (by which I mean I would not expect the elasticity of real aggregate demand with respect to the real wage rate to be very large). The simplest sort of Keynesian model of income determination makes real consumption a function of real income and real investment more or less exogenous. In that case, aggregate demand is independent of the real wage. No one would justify so crude a model of income determination these days. But if it is even a fair first approximation, the real wage effect must belong to the second approximation, or even perhaps the third. Not much is known in fact about differences among the marginal propensities to spend different sorts of incomes, primarily because there are no official data on disposable income by income-type. In the absence of evidence, the safe course is probably to regard aggregate demand as a gently increasing function of the real wage.

Aggregate supply presumably goes the other way. In the short run, with the economy's stock of capital goods given, the aggregate supply of output for given money wage and price level is the volume of real output industry as a whole is

41

willing to produce. For a given money wage, aggregate supply will be higher the higher the commodity price level. The wage bill is the largest element of prime cost; at a given money wage, a higher price level permits profitable operation of older, less productive, higher cost, plant and equipment. If the price level were lower or the money wage higher, some marginal capacity would be unable to earn the required quasi-rents and would be shifted into idleness. There would be a corresponding reduction in employment. One supposes, therefore, that the aggregate supply of real output is an increasing function of P/W, the price level in wage-units, or a decreasing function of $W/P = V$, the real wage.

It follows that whenever there is excess demand, so that actual output is determined on the supply side, current output and employment will be lower the higher the real wage.

There have not been many—perhaps not any—attempts to estimate aggregate supply functions econometrically. In principle, an estimate of the aggregate production function plus an assumption about the average 'degree of monopoly' will determine an aggregate supply curve. There is a difficulty of interpretation, however. Most attempts to estimate aggregate production functions seem to be getting at long-period relations. In the present context, we want a short-run curve relating fluctuations in output and the corresponding variations in employment, with variations in effective demand the prime mover. One doesn't know if long-run production functions contain the right sort of information.

There can be no harm in an example. Suppose that $Y = N^h$ in the short run, where N is employment and h is between zero and one. (If the traditional Cobb-Douglas parameters hold for short-run fluctuations of output and employment, then h is about $\frac{3}{4}$.) Then marginal cost is W/hN^{h-1} and we can set $P = mW/hN^{h-1}$, where m is the mark-up of price over marginal cost, which I shall suppose insensitive to small variations in Y. It now follows that the aggregate supply function is $Y = (mV/h)^{h/h-1}$. For instance, if $h = \frac{3}{4}$, Y is proportional to V^{-3}; if $h = 0.6$, Y is proportional to $V^{-3/2}$. It seems plausible that the proper short-run value of h

42

might be smaller than the proper long-run value, but nothing much depends on that.

At very low real wage rates, one would suppose that aggregate demand considerations predominate. There is plenty of spare capacity and unemployment. Real output would be higher if there were a market for it at the going level of prices. In this state of affairs, a higher real wage corresponds to a higher level of output. The higher real wage will expand aggregate demand. It will also reduce margins, but since the limit to output is on the demand side, output will expand. If aggregate demand is only a very slowly increasing function of the real wage rate, then this effect will be small.

At very high real wage rates, there is more likely to be excess demand and aggregate supply considerations will predominate. Real output would be higher if it could be profitably produced at the going wage-price configuration; by definition there is an unsatisfied market at the going price. In this state of affairs, a higher real wage corresponds to a lower level of output; marginal capacity will be priced out of operation. (Of course, when there is excess demand both wages and prices will be rising rapidly; but when the level of output is supply-determined, it will respond to the ratio of P to W. There are undoubtedly lags and frictions in this mechanism, but I shall ignore them. They get a more careful treatment in the article referred to earlier.)

The situation is represented in Diagram 3, with the real wage V measured horizontally and real output Y measured vertically. The curve we have just been discussing has an inverted-V shape; but we reserve the possibility that the rising branch is relatively flat. On this Diagram 3 superimpose a horizontal line at $Y = Y^*$, the level of output at which the trade-off relations generate equal rates of increase of W and P, and so a constant V. There are now two main cases according as v is an increasing or decreasing function of Y. Special cases arise when the horizontal at Y^* intersects only one branch of the Y–V curve, or lies wholly above it. These are also illustrated in Diagram 3.

The diagram works as follows. The momentary state of the

economy is summarized by two variables, V and Y. By assumption, V amd Y always lie on the humped curve that relates the level of output to the real wage rate. The direction

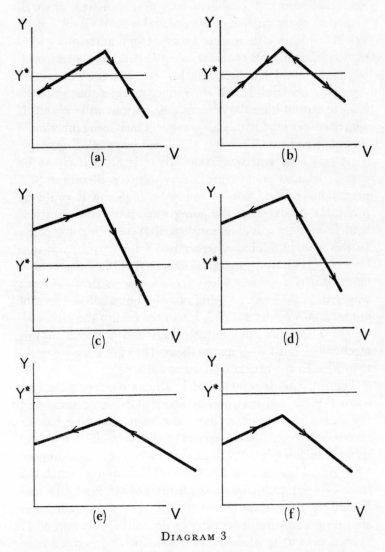

DIAGRAM 3

in which V is changing comes from the combined trade-off equations. In case (a) v is an increasing function of Y, so that V is decreasing (v is negative) below Y^* and increasing (v is

44

positive) above $\varUpsilon^*$. In case (b) v is a decreasing function of $\varUpsilon$, so V rises below $\varUpsilon^*$ and falls above $\varUpsilon^*$. In all cases, $\varUpsilon$ moves as it must move to stay on the curve. The arrows show what happens.

In part (a) of the diagram there are two possible situations with constant real wage; that is to say, there are two points on the $\varUpsilon$–V curve where $\varUpsilon = \varUpsilon^*$ and $v = 0$. But the left-hand one is unstable. The arrows indicate that, if the economy is disturbed from that point, it will move further away, either into a situation of falling real wage and falling output or into a stage of rising real wage which leads to the right-hand constant-V point. This one is stable; if the economy is disturbed slightly in either direction, it will return to its initial configuration. Part (b) of the diagram is similar except that the left-hand constant-V situation is the stable one.

Parts (c) and (d) of the diagram illustrate cases in which the left-hand excess-supply equilibria disappear and only the excess-demand equilibria remain. In (c) there is a stable configuration with constant real wage; in case (d) there is not. In principle, there are symmetrical cases in which only the excess-supply equilibrium remains; but those cases are unlikely if aggregate demand is only weakly dependent on the real wage. Parts (e) and (f) illustrate situations with no equilibrium point.

The interesting situations are those illustrated in (a) and (b). They show how a closed model can dissipate the paradox with which I introduced this lecture. In part (a) of the diagram there is a stable equilibrium (at least in the short run) with excess demand for output. Almost certainly there is inflation; the price level and money wage are rising. But they are rising at the same rate so that the real wage is not changing. The distribution of national income is also constant. The parameters of the trade-off equations determine the actual rate of inflation, and they help to determine the equilibrium level of real output and the real wage. But whatever the parameters of the trade-off equations, regular inflation can cheat neither wage nor nonwage income systematically.

In the situation of part (b) the short run equilibrium is

45

demand-limited; there is excess supply in commodity markets and presumably unemployment in the labor market. The diagram doesn't say whether the price level is deflating or inflating. That can be found out from either trade-off equation. Such situations do in fact seem to arise, with the price

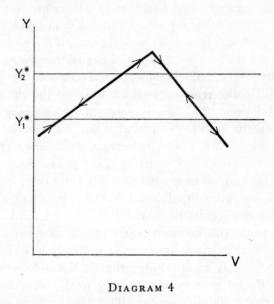

DIAGRAM 4

level actually rising despite the existence of what any reasonable man would call excess capacity and unemployment. That observation was the starting point for this series of lectures.[1]

I will conclude with one further possibility. Earlier, in Diagram 2, I mentioned that in plausible circumstances

[1] Diagram 3b has one unacceptable implication as it stands. Suppose the aggregate demand schedule were to rise (by virtue of government spending, say). The upward-sloping part of the Y–V curve would shift upward. The new short-run equilibrium position would have a lower real wage, but the *same* level of real output Y^*. The implausible result, that a shift in aggregate demand has no effect on real output in an underemployment equilibrium, is an implication of the assumption that $v = 0$ implies $Y = Y^*$. If the relation between v and Y involves other variables as well, in particular V, then the implausible implication disappears. I have made v depend only on Y^* simply as an expository simplification.

46

there might be two levels of income at which the real wage would stabilize. That leads to Diagram 4, which contains four possible equilibrium points, two of which are stable and two unstable. In such a case, depending on where it 'begins', the economy may tend in the short run either to an excess-demand equilibrium or to one with excess supply. The interesting possibility emerges that the economy might be jolted out of an underemployment equilibrium and transferred to a new 'initial position' from which it might find its way to an inflationary excess-demand equilibrium, or *vice versa*.

APPENDIX NOTE 1

Mr. John Hutton of the University of York suggested an alternative estimation procedure. From the trade-off equation

$$p_t = ax_t + by_t + cp^* + u_t$$

and the definition of adaptive expectations

$$p_t^* = (1 - \theta)p_{t-1}^* + \theta p_{t-1}$$

one easily deduces (in the Koyck-transform manner) the equation

$$p_t = a(x_t - (1 - \theta)x_{t-1}) + b(y_t - (1 - \theta)y_{t-1})$$
$$+ (1 - \theta + c\theta)p_{t-1} + u_t - (1 - \theta)u_{t-1}.$$

Here x_t and y_t are shorthand for any independent variables, and u_t is the residual in the trade-off equation.

I have estimated this equation by taking trial values of θ and using ordinary least squares. The implied coefficient c is easily recovered. This method is more appropriate than my original one when $u_t - \theta u_{t-1}$ is more nearly serially uncorrelated than u_t, which is not implausible.

I will not reproduce all the results, but just give the estimated trade-off equation for two values of θ. The highest correlation $(R^2 = \cdot 9272)$ occurs for $\theta = 0 \cdot 4$ with the equation

$$p = \cdot 0045 + \cdot 2972w + \cdot 3674\bar{r} + \cdot 3019fs + \cdot 0048NCU$$
$$(2 \cdot 245) \quad (4 \cdot 287) \quad (3 \cdot 667) \quad (1 \cdot 793) \quad (0 \cdot 923)$$
$$+ \cdot 0276K - \cdot 0021G + \cdot 1269p^*.$$
$$(6 \cdot 304) \quad (0 \cdot 707)$$

The correlation falls away very slowly on either side of $\theta = 0 \cdot 4$, so that, as in the text, θ itself is not very well estimated.

For example, the choice $\theta = 0 \cdot 7$ reduces R^2 only to $\cdot 9225$ and yields the equation

$$p = \cdot 0059 + \cdot 2348w + \cdot 2487\bar{r} + \cdot 4359fs + \cdot 0075NCU$$
$$(2 \cdot 197) \quad (3 \cdot 109) \quad (3 \cdot 183) \quad (2 \cdot 609) \quad (1 \cdot 489)$$
$$+ \cdot 0187K - \cdot 0033G + \cdot 3224p^*.$$
$$(4 \cdot 126) \quad (1 \cdot 600)$$

These two regressions are to be compared with Table 1 of the text. There are some differences. For instance, the coefficient of the normalized change in farm prices is substantially lower in these alternative estimates. Capacity utilization and the 'guideposts dummy' fail of statistical significance in this estimate using $\theta = 0.4$, but do rather better when $\theta = 0.7$. It is interesting that the alternative equation with $\theta = 0.7$ has coefficients much like those of the row of Table 1 with $\theta = 0.4$.

The main observation I want to make is simply that these regressions give somewhat *lower* estimates of the coefficient of p^* than those in Table 1. There is still no statistical case that the coefficient of p^* is near unity, hence the strict expectations hypothesis fails with these estimates too. (I have not given t-statistics for the coefficients of p^* because what is actually estimated is the coefficient of p_{t-1} in the combined regression. Its standard error is not the standard error of c. Notice that if $c = 1$, that coefficient (i.e. $1 - \theta + c\theta$) becomes unity for all θ. The estimated coefficient of p_{t-1} is always many standard errors away from unity, except when θ is near zero, which doesn't help the expectations hypothesis.)

APPENDIX NOTE 2

Briscoe, O'Brien and Smyth ('The Measurement of Capacity: A Preliminary Investigation', Graduate Centre for Management Studies, Birmingham, 1968, mimeographed) generate six alternative quarterly measures of capacity utilization with a coverage that extends beyond manufacturing but falls short of the whole economy. Two of the measures are modelled on the Wharton School series for the United States, two are based on 'capacity multipliers', and two on a primitive production function. Since these lectures were written, I have tried out the various series in quarterly regressions like the one reported on page 23. The results are broadly similar to those I found using the Paish series. It seems, therefore, that the differences between annual and quarterly regressions do not stem from peculiarities of the capacity-utilization variable.

There is no need to report the alternative results in detail, but I can characterize them briefly.

The Paish series gave the best fit, but only marginally better than the Wharton-type series which were, in turn, slightly better than the others. The better of the two Wharton-type series, like the Paish series, fit best for $\theta = 0.7$.

The regression shown on page 23 gives p^* a coefficient of 0.8, rather close to one. All the alternative regressions give p^* a coefficient very near 0.7, rather further from one. The better of the two Wharton-type series has another interesting property: it gives ulc a coefficient of 0.11 instead of 0.08. But the two changes together leave the implied long-run effect of ulc, when expectations are fully adapted, more or less unchanged.